THE GODS OF WINTER

1 9 9 1

THE GODS
OF WINTER

POEMS BY

DANA GIOIA

• • •

GRAYWOLF PRESS : SAINT PAUL

For Mark Jarman —
della nobile brigata,

Dana Gioia

The following poems, sometimes in earlier versions, appeared in the following publications: "Places to Return" in *Connoisseur;* "The Homecoming," in *Crosscurrents;* "Veteran's Cemetery" in the *Formalist;* "Counting the Children," "Maze Without a Minotaur," and "Los Angeles After the Rain" in the *Hudson Review;* "Prayer" and "Planting a Sequoia" in the *New Criterion;* "All Souls'," "Equations of the Light," and "Orchestra" in the *New Yorker;* "Becoming a Redwood" in the *Paris Review;* "Night Watch," "The Gods of Winter," "On Approaching Forty," "The Next Poem," "My Confessional Sestina," and "Speaking of Love" in *Poetry;* "News from Nineteen Eighty-Four" in the *Reaper;* "The Song" in *Sequoia;* "The Silence of the Poets" in *Southwest Review;* "Rough Country," "Cleared Away," and "Guide to the Other Gallery" in *Verse;* "Money" in the *Wallace Stevens Journal.*

The first seven poems of this collection were printed in a limited edition titled, *Planting a Sequoia* by Aralia Press; "Equations of the Light" and "Maze Without a Minotaur" were published as *Two Poems / Due Poesie* by Linda Samson-Talleur; "Los Angeles After the Rain" was reprinted in *Anthology of Magazine Verse and Yearbook of American Poetry, 1986-1988;* "Places to Return" and "All Souls'" appeared in the 1989 edition. The author thanks these editors and printers for their support.

Publication of this volume is made possible in part by a grant provided by the Minnesota State Arts Board, through an appropriation by the Minnesota State Legislature, and by a grant from the National Endowment for the Arts. Additional support has been provided by generous contributions from foundations, corporations, and individuals, and through a major grant from the Northwest Area Foundation. Graywolf Press is a member agency of United Arts, Saint Paul, and is a recipient of a McKnight Foundation award administered by the Minnesota State Arts Board.

Published by GRAYWOLF PRESS
2402 University Avenue, Saint Paul, Minnesota 55114

First printing
9 8 7 6 5 4 3 2
Library of Congress Cataloging-in-Publication Data
Gioia, Dana.
The gods of winter : poems / by Dana Gioia.
p. cm.
ISBN 1-55597-147-4 : $22.95
ISBN 1-55597-148-2 (pbk.) : $9.95
I. Title.
PS3557.I5215G64 1991
811'.54—dc20 90-24790

In Memory of My Son

Briefest of joys, our life together.

CONTENTS

I.

II.

III.

IV.

V.

· I ·

Farewell, thou child of my right hand, and joy.

— BEN JONSON

PRAYER

Echo of the clocktower, footstep
in the alleyway, sweep
of the wind sifting the leaves.

Jeweller of the spiderweb, connoisseur
of autumn's opulence, blade of lightning
harvesting the sky.

Keeper of the small gate, choreographer
of entrances and exits, midnight
whisper travelling the wires.

Seducer, healer, deity or thief,
I will see you soon enough –
in the shadow of the rainfall,

in the brief violet darkening a sunset –
but until then I pray watch over him
as a mountain guards its covert ore

and the harsh falcon its flightless young.

ALL SOULS'

Suppose there is no heaven and no hell,
And that the dead can never leave the earth,
That, as the body rots, the soul breaks free,
Weak and disabled in its second birth.

And then invisible, rising to the light,
Each finds a world it cannot touch or hear,
Where colors fade and, if the soul cries out,
The silence stays unbroken in the air.

How flat the ocean seems without its roar,
Without the sting of salt, the bracing gust.
The sunset blurs into a grayish haze.
The morning snowfall is a cloud of dust.

The pines that they revisit have no scent.
They cannot feel the needled forest floor.
Crossing the stream, they watch the current flow
Unbroken as they step down from the shore.

They want their voices to become the wind –
Intangible like them – to match its cry,
Howling in treetops, covering the moon,
Tumbling the storm clouds in a rain-swept sky.

But they are silent as a rising mist,
A smudge of smoke dissolving in the air.
They watch the shadows lengthen on the grass.
The pallor of the rose is their despair.

NIGHT WATCH

For my uncle, Theodore Ortiz, U.S.M.M.

I think of you standing on the sloping deck
as the freighter pulls away from the coast of China,
the last lights of Asia disappearing in the fog,
and the engine's drone dissolving in the old
monotony of waves slapping up against the hull.

Leaning on the rails, looking eastward to America
across the empty weeks of ocean,
how carefully you must have planned your life,
so much of it already wasted on the sea,
the vast country of your homelessness.

Macao. Vladivostok. Singapore.
Dante read by shiplamp on the bridge.
The names of fellow sailors lost in war.
These memories will die with you,
but tonight they rise up burning in your mind

interweaving like gulls crying in the wake,
like currents on a chart, like gulfweed
swirling in a star-soaked sea, and interchangeable
as all the words for night – *la notte, noche, Nacht, nuit,*
each sound half-foreign, half-familiar, like America.

For now you know that mainland best from dreams.
Your dead mother turning toward you slowly,
always on the edge of words, yet always
silent as the suffering madonna of a shrine.
Or your father pounding his fist against the wall.

There are so many ways to waste a life.
Why choose between these icons of unhappiness,

when there is the undisguised illusion of the sea,
the comfort of old books and solitude to fill
the long night watch, the endless argument of waves?

Breathe in that dark and tangible air, for in a few weeks
you will be dead, burned beyond recognition,
left as a headstone in the unfamiliar earth
with no one to ask, neither wife nor children,
why your thin ashes have been buried here

and not scattered on the shifting gray Pacific.

VETERANS' CEMETERY

The ceremonies of the day have ceased,
Abandoned to the ragged crow's parade.
The flags unravel in the caterpillar's feast.
The wreaths collapse onto the stones they shade.

How quietly doves gather by the gate
Like souls who have no heaven and no hell.
The patient grass reclaims its lost estate
Where one stone angel stands as sentinel.

The voices whispering in the burning leaves,
Faint and inhuman, what can they desire
When every season feeds upon the past,
And summer's green ignites the autumn's fire?

The afternoon's a single thread of light
Sewn through the tatters of a leafless willow,
As one by one the branches fade from sight,
And time curls up like paper turning yellow.

THE SONG

How shall I hold my soul that it
does not touch yours? How shall I lift
it over you to other things?
If it would only sink below
into the dark like some lost thing
or slumber in some quiet place
which did not echo your soft heart's beat.
But all that ever touched us — you and me —
touched us together
                    like a bow
that from two strings could draw one voice.
On what instrument were we strung?
And to what player did we sing
our interrupted song?

(After Rilke)

THE GODS OF WINTER

Storm on storm, snow on drifting snowfall,
shifting its shape, flurrying in moonlight,
bright and ubiquitous,
profligate March squanders its wealth.
The world is annihilated and remade
with only us as witnesses.

Briefest of joys, our life together,
this brittle flower twisting toward the light
even as it dies, no more permanent
for being perfect. Time will melt away
triumphant winter, and even your touch
prove the unpossessable jewel of ice.

And vanish like this unseasonable storm
drifting there beyond the windows where even
the cluttered rooftops now lie soft and luminous
like a storybook view of paradise.
Why not believe these suave messengers
of starlight? Morning will make

their brightness blinding, and the noon insist
that only legend saves the beautiful. But if
the light confides how one still winter must
arrive without us, then our eternity
is only this white storm, the whisper
of your breath, the deities of this quiet night.

PLANTING A SEQUOIA

All afternoon my brothers and I have worked in the orchard,
Digging this hole, laying you into it, carefully packing the soil.
Rain blackened the horizon, but cold winds kept it over the Pacific,
And the sky above us stayed the dull gray
Of an old year coming to an end.

In Sicily a father plants a tree to celebrate his first son's birth –
An olive or a fig tree – a sign that the earth has one more life to bear.
I would have done the same, proudly laying new stock into my father's
        orchard,
A green sapling rising among the twisted apple boughs,
A promise of new fruit in other autumns.

But today we kneel in the cold planting you, our native giant,
Defying the practical custom of our fathers,
Wrapping in your roots a lock of hair, a piece of an infant's birth cord,
All that remains above earth of a first-born son,
A few stray atoms brought back to the elements.

We will give you what we can – our labor and our soil,
Water drawn from the earth when the skies fail,
Nights scented with the ocean fog, days softened by the circuit of
        bees.
We plant you in the corner of the grove, bathed in western light,
A slender shoot against the sunset.

And when our family is no more, all of his unborn brothers dead,
Every niece and nephew scattered, the house torn down,
His mother's beauty ashes in the air,
I want you to stand among strangers, all young and ephemeral to you,
Silently keeping the secret of your birth.

· II ·

What did I know, what did I know
of love's austere and lonely offices?

— ROBERT HAYDEN

COUNTING THE CHILDREN

"This must have been her bedroom, Mr. Choi.
It's hard to tell. The only other time
I came back here was when I found her body."

Neither of us belonged there. She lived next door.
I was the accountant sent out by the State
To take an inventory of the house.

When someone wealthy dies without a will,
The court sends me to audit the estate.
They know that strangers trust a man who listens.

The neighbor led me down an unlit hall.
We came up to a double door and stopped.
She whispered as if someone else were near.

"She used to wander around town at night
And rifle through the trash. We all knew that.
But what we didn't know about was *them*."

She stepped inside and fumbled for a switch.
It didn't work, but light leaked through the curtains.
"Come in," she said. "I want to show you hell."

I walked into a room of wooden shelves
Stretching from floor to ceiling, wall to wall,
With smaller shelves arranged along the center.

A crowd of faces looked up silently.
Shoulder to shoulder, standing all in rows,
Hundreds of dolls were lining every wall.

Not a collection anyone would want –
Just ordinary dolls salvaged from the trash
With dozens of each kind all set together.

Some battered, others missing arms and legs,
Shelf after shelf of the same dusty stare
As if despair could be assuaged by order.

They looked like sisters huddling in the dark,
Forgotten brides abandoned at the altar,
Their veils turned yellow, dresses stiff and soiled.

Rows of discarded little girls and babies –
Some naked, others dressed for play – they wore
Whatever lives their owners left them in.

Where were the children who promised them love?
The small, caressing hands, the lips which whispered
Secrets in the dark? Once they were woken,

Each by name. Now they have become each other –
Anonymous except for injury,
The beautiful and headless side by side.

Was this where all lost childhoods go? These dim
Abandoned rooms, these crude arrangements staged
For settled dust and shadow, left to prove

That all affection is outgrown, or show
The uniformity of our desire?
How dismal someone else's joy can be.

I stood between the speechless shelves and knew
Dust has a million lives, the heart has one.
I turned away and started my report.

That night I dreamt of working on a ledger,
A book so large it stretched across my desk,
Thousands of numbers running down each page.

I knew I had to settle the account,
Yet as I tried to calculate the total,
The numbers started slipping down the page,

Suddenly breaking up like Scrabble letters
Brushed into a box to end a game,
Each strained-for word uncoupled back to nil.

But as I tried to add them back together
And hold each number on the thin green line
Where it belonged, I realized that now

Nothing I did would ever fit together.
In my hands even $2 + 2 + 2$
No longer equaled anything at all.

And then I saw my father there beside me.
He asked me why I couldn't find the sum.
He held my daughter crying in his arms.

My family stood behind him in a row,
Uncles and aunts, cousins I'd never seen,
My grandparents from China and their parents,

All of my family, living and dead,
A line that stretched as far as I could see.
Even the strangers called to me by name.

And now I saw I wasn't at my desk
But working on the coffin of my daughter,
And she would die unless I found the sum.

But I had lost too many of the numbers.
They tumbled to the floor and blazed on fire.
I saw the dolls then — screaming in the flames.

III.

When I awoke, I sat up straight in bed.
The sweaty sheet was twisted in my hands.
My heart was pounding. Had I really screamed?

But no, my wife was still asleep beside me.
I got up quietly and found my robe,
Knowing I couldn't fall asleep again.

Then groping down the unlit hall, I saw
A soft-edged light beneath my daughter's door.
It was the night-light plugged in by her bed.

And I remembered when she was a baby,
How often I would get up in the night
And creep into that room to watch her sleep.

I never told my wife how many times
I came to check each night — or that I was
Always afraid of what I might discover.

I felt so helpless standing by her crib,
Watching the quiet motions of her breath
In the half-darkness of the faint night-light.

How delicate this vessel in our care,
This gentle soul we summoned to the world,
A life we treasured but could not protect.

This was the terror I could not confess –
Not even to my wife – and it was the joy
My daughter had no words to understand.

So standing at my pointless watch each night
In the bare nursery we had improvised,
I learned the loneliness that we call love.

IV.

But I gave up those vigils years ago.
My daughter's seven now, and I don't worry –
At least no more than any father does.

But waking up last night after the dream,
Trembling in the hall, looking at her door,
I let myself be drawn into her room.

She was asleep – the blankets softly rising
And falling with each breath, the faint light tracing
The sleek unfoldings of her long black hair.

Then suddenly I felt myself go numb.
And though you won't believe that an accountant
Can have a vision, I will tell you mine.

Each of us thinks our own child beautiful,
But watching her and marveling at the sheer
Smoothness of skin without a scar or blemish,

I saw beyond my daughter to all children,
And, though elated, still I felt confused
Because I wondered why I never sensed

That thrill of joy when looking at adults
No matter how refined or beautiful,
Why lust or envy always intervened.

There is no *tabula rasa* for the soul.
Each spirit, be it infant, bird or flower,
Comes to the world perfected and complete,

And only time proves its unraveling.
But I'm digressing from my point, my vision.
What I meant to ask is merely this:

What if completion comes only in beginnings?
The naked tree exploding into flower?
And all our prim assumptions about time

Prove wrong? What if we cannot read the future
Because our destiny moves back in time,
And only memory speaks prophetically?

We long for immortality, a soul
To rise up flaming from the body's dust.
I know that it exists. I felt it there,

Perfect and eternal in the way
That only numbers are, intangible but real,
Infinitely divisible yet whole.

But we do not possess it in ourselves.
We die, and it abides, and we are one
With all our ancestors, while it divides

Over and over, common to us all,
The ancient face returning in the child,
The distant arms embracing us, the salt

Of our blind origins filling our veins.
I stood confused beside my daughter's bed
Surprised to find the room around me dim.

Then glancing at the bookshelf in the corner,
I saw she'd lined her dolls up in a row.
Three little girls were sitting in the dark.

Their sharp glass eyes surveyed me with contempt.
They recognized me only as a rival,
The one whose world would keep no place for them.

I felt like holding them tight in my arms,
Promising I would never let them go,
But they would trust no promises of mine.

I feared that if I touched one, it would scream.

· III ·

*I think there is a spirit of place,
a presence asking to be expressed.*

—JOHN HAINES

ROUGH COUNTRY

Give me a landscape made of obstacles,
of steep hills and jutting glacial rock,
where the low-running streams are quick to flood
the grassy fields and bottomlands.
                              A place
no engineers can master – where the roads
must twist like tendrils up the mountainside
on narrow cliffs where boulders block the way.

Where tall black trunks of lightning-scalded pine
push through the tangled woods to make a roost
for hawks and swarming crows.
                              And sharp inclines
where twisting through the thorn-thick underbrush,
scratched and exhausted, one turns suddenly

to find an unexpected waterfall,
not half a mile from the nearest road,
a spot so hard to reach that no one comes –

a hiding place, a shrine for dragonflies
and nesting jays, a sign that there is still
one piece of property that won't be owned.

CLEARED AWAY

Around the corner there may be a man
who shop by shop, block by ruined block,
still sees the neighborhood which once was here,

who, standing in the empty lot, can hear
the vacancies of brick and broken glass
suddenly come to life again, who feels

the steps materialize beneath his feet
as he ascends the shattered tenement,
which rises with him in the open air –

story by story, out of memory,
filled with the smells of dinners on the stove
and the soft laughter of the assembled dead.

ON APPROACHING FORTY

The thought pursues me through this dreary town
where the wind sweeps down from the high plateau
and where a diving chimney swift can cut
the slender thread of mountains far away.

So soon come forty years of restlessness,
of tedium, of unexpected joy,
quick as a gust of wind in March is quick
to scatter light and rain. Soon come delays,
snatched from the straining hands of those I love,
torn from my haunts, the customs of my years
suddenly crushed to make me understand.
The tree of sorrow shakes its branches. . . .

The years rise like a swarm around my shoulders.
Nothing has been in vain. This is the work
which all complete together and alone,
the living and the dead, to penetrate
the impenetrable world, down open roads,
down mineshafts of discovery and loss,
and learned from many loves or only one,
from father down to son – till all is clear.

And having said this, I can start out now,
easy in the eternal company
of all things living, of all things dead,
to disappear in either dust or fire
if any fire endures beyond its flame.

(From the Italian of Mario Luzi)

PLACES TO RETURN

There are landscapes one can own,
bright rooms which look out to the sea,
tall houses where beyond the window
day after day the same dark river
turns slowly through the hills, and there
are homesteads perched on mountaintops
whose cool white caps outlast the spring.

And there are other places which,
although we did not stay for long,
stick in the mind and call us back —
a valley visited one spring
where walking through an apple orchard
we breathed its blossoms with the air.
Return seems like a sacrament.

Then there are landscapes one has lost —
the brown hills circling a wide bay
I watched each afternoon one summer
talking to friends who now are dead.
I like to think I could go back again
and stand out on the balcony,
dizzy with a sense of *déjà vu*.

But coming up these steps to you
at just that moment when the moon,
magnificently full and bright
behind the lattice-work of clouds,
seems almost set upon the rooftops
it illuminates, how shall I
ever summon it again?

This is the hall of broken limbs
Where splintered marble athletes lie
Beside the arms of cherubim.
Nothing is ever thrown away.

These butterflies are set in rows.
So small and gray inside their case
They look alike now. I suppose
Death makes most creatures commonplace.

These portraits here of the unknown
Are hung three high, frame piled on frame.
Each potent soul who craved renown,
Immortalized without a name.

Here are the shelves of unread books,
Millions of pages turning brown.
Visitors wander through the stacks,
But no one ever takes one down.

I wish I were a better guide.
There's so much more that you should see.
Rows of bottles with nothing inside.
Displays of locks which have no key.

You'd like to go? I wish you could.
This room has such a peaceful view.
Look at that case of antique wood
Without a label. It's for you.

NEWS FROM NINETEEN EIGHTY-FOUR

for James Fenton

The great offensive in the East began
this morning as our forces overran
the enemy's positions. Total victory
is now expected within weeks! The Spring
Youth Festival will be delayed by an
impromptu demonstration of support.
Arrests continue at the Ministry.
The weekly coffee ration will remain
at sixty grams. More news in half an hour.

Arrests continue at the Ministry
where ten high-ranking members have confessed
to crimes against the People. Late last night
news of another massive victory
along the Eastern front. "The end's in sight,"
our Leader commented as he released
the record figures of the summer harvest.
Impromptu demonstrations of support
occurred throughout the capital. More news at ten.

Fighting is still intense along the front
as the cold weather stalls the enemy's
feeble offensive. Now that the bombardment
of the capital has ceased, the execution
of draft evaders will resume tonight
in Freedom Square. All rations have been raised
with coffee now at thirty grams. Production
goals have been surpassed in tin and bauxite.
Morale among the volunteers is high.

The fires at the docks have been contained
with suspects netted in a late-night sweep.
The enemy's offensive in the East
has been repulsed at great cost. But morale
among the senior volunteers is high.
The Worker's Festival began last night
with execution of trade dissidents.
Spring coffee rations climb to twenty grams.
Arrests continue at the Ministry.

is something to be grateful for.
Once there were so many books, so many poets.
All the masterpieces one could never read,
indistinguishable even then
among the endless shelves of the unreadable.

Some claim the best stopped writing first.
For the others, no one noted when or why.
A few observers voiced their mild regret
about another picturesque, unprofitable craft
that progress had irrevocably doomed.

And what was lost? No one now can judge.
But we still have music, art, and film,
diversions enough for a busy people.
And even poetry for those who want it.
The old books, those the young have not defaced,
are still kept somewhere,
stacked in their dusty rows.

And a few old men may visit from time to time
to run their hands across the spines
and reminisce,
but no one ever comes to read
or would know how.

MY CONFESSIONAL SESTINA

Let me confess. I'm sick of these sestinas
written by youngsters in poetry workshops
for the delectation of their fellow students,
and then published in little magazines
that no one reads, not even the contributors
who at least in this omission show some taste.

Is this merely a matter of personal taste?
I don't think so. Most sestinas
are such dull affairs. Just ask the contributors
the last time they finished one outside of a workshop,
even the poignant one on herpes in that new little magazine
edited by their most brilliant fellow student.

Let's be honest. It has become a form for students,
an exercise to build technique rather than taste
and the official entry blank into the little magazines –
because despite its reputation, a passable sestina
isn't very hard to write, even for kids in workshops
who care less about being poets than contributors.

Granted nowadays everyone is a contributor.
My barber is currently a student
in a rigorous correspondence school workshop.
At lesson six he can already taste
success having just placed his own sestina
in a national tonsorial magazine.

Who really cares about most little magazines?
Eventually not even their own contributors
who having published a few preliminary sestinas

send their work East to prove they're no longer students.
They need to be recognized as the new arbiters of taste
so they can teach their own graduate workshops.

Where will it end? This grim cycle of workshops
churning out poems for little magazines
no one honestly finds to their taste?
This ever-lengthening column of contributors
scavenging the land for more students
teaching them to write their boot-camp sestinas?

Perhaps there is an afterlife where all contributors
have two workshops, a tasteful little magazine, and sexy students
who worshipfully memorize their every sestina.

MONEY

Money is a kind of poetry.
— WALLACE STEVENS

Money, the long green,
cash, stash, rhino, jack
or just plain dough.

Chock it up, fork it over,
shell it out. Watch it
burn holes through pockets.

To be made of it! To have it
to burn! Greenbacks, double eagles,
megabucks and Ginnie Maes.

It greases the palm, feathers a nest,
holds heads above water,
makes both ends meet.

Money breeds money.
Gathering interest, compounding daily.
Always in circulation.

Money. You don't know where it's been,
but you put it where your mouth is.
And it talks.

THE NEXT POEM

How much better it seems now
than when it is finally done –
the unforgettable first line,
the cunning way the stanzas run.

The rhymes soft-spoken and suggestive
are barely audible at first,
an appetite not yet acknowledged
like the inkling of a thirst.

While gradually the form appears
as each line is coaxed aloud –
the architecture of a room
seen from the middle of a crowd.

The music that of common speech
but slanted so that each detail
sounds unexpected as a sharp
inserted in a simple scale.

No jumble box of imagery
dumped glumly in the reader's lap
or elegantly packaged junk
the unsuspecting must unwrap.

But words that could direct a friend
precisely to an unknown place,
those few unshakeable details
that no confusion can erase.

And the real subject left unspoken
but unmistakable to those
who don't expect a jungle parrot
in the black and white of prose.

How much better it seems now
than when it is finally written.
How hungrily one waits to feel
the bright lure seized, the old hook bitten.

· IV ·

How shall I speak of doom, and ours in special,
But as of something altogether common?

—DONALD JUSTICE

THE HOMECOMING

I watched your headlights coming up the drive
and thought, "Thank God, it's over." Do you know
I waited up all night for you – with only
the bugs for company? I tried to watch them
beating their wings against the windowpanes
but only saw my own reflection on the glass,
blurry and bodiless against the black.
I finally passed the time remembering
what it was like to grow up in this house.

This little parlor hasn't changed a bit
in twenty years. Those china figurines
along the mantelpiece, the ivory fan,
the green silk pillows puffed up on the couch
were sitting in exactly the same place
when I first came. And that pathetic print
of Jesus smiling by the telephone –
even the music in the piano stool.
These things should have been thrown away by now
or put up in the attic and forgotten.

But you aren't interested in family heirlooms.
I know the reason that you're here is me.
I won't resist. I'm ready to go back.
Tomorrow you'll be heroes in the paper –
KILLER NABBED AT FOSTER MOTHER'S HOME.
But first there's something else you need to know.
Look in the other room. No need to hurry.

She raised me, but she wasn't family.
I don't know how she first got custody,
except that no one really wanted me.
My father disappeared when I was three.
I don't remember him. Then the next year
my mother took off, too. After she left
I saw her only once — by accident —
at the State Fair one Sunday afternoon
when I was twelve. I went without permission.
I should have been attending Sunday School
to find salvation over milk and cookies,
but I had sneaked away. I couldn't stand
another dreary day of Jesus. I knew
there would be hell to pay when I got home.
Still I was happy, wandering through the booths,
drunk with the noise, the music, and the rides,
not feeling lonely any more but merged
into those joyful crowds who didn't care
that it was Sunday. Moving in their midst,
for once I felt I wasn't different,
that we all shared a common world of grace
where simple daylight could bring happiness.

Then suddenly I saw her at a booth,
my mother, talking to some man, and she
was holding a stuffed animal they'd won,
chatting with it in the sort of baby talk
that lovers use. At first I wasn't sure
if it was her. I started to call out,
but then she noticed I was watching her.

And for an instant we stood face to face.
I knew from pictures it was her. And she
paused for a moment, staring absently,

her beautiful face troubled by the thought
of something brushing over her unseen.
A puzzled look, a moment's hesitation,
and then a smile as if she realized
that her imagination could play tricks.

She smiled and winked at me, the intimacy
of strangers at a summer fair, a smile
without the slightest trace of recognition.
I turned and ran the whole way home,
and when the old bitch paddled me that night
for missing church, for once I didn't mind.

III.

God didn't care. He saw where I belonged.
She told me years ago how everyone
would either go to Heaven or to Hell.
God knew it all, and nothing you could do
would make a difference. I asked her how
a person knew where he was chosen for.
She said, "A person always knows inside."
She asked me suddenly – for the first time –
if I were saved. I couldn't give an answer.
"Look in your heart," she told me. "Look for Jesus."

All night I lay in bed and thought about it.
I tried to pray, but mostly I just kept
imagining my heart, how dry it was
and empty like a shell that long ago
someone walking on the beach had found
sparkling in the surf. And now it lies
forgotten in a cluttered dresser drawer
where no one sees or touches it again.
And if you ever put it to your ear,
you wouldn't hear the crash of ocean waves.

All you would feel is the harshness of bone.
All you would hear is a sigh of loneliness
so small that you could hold it in your hand.

That night I knew that I would go to Hell,
and it would be a place just like my room —
dark, suffocating, with its door shut tight,
and even if my mother were there too,
she wouldn't find me. I would always be alone.

IV.

The next night I ran away. I ran for miles
through fields and farmlands without any aim.
It was so dark I couldn't see my way.
Then pushing through a cornfield, suddenly
I tripped and slid into some kind of hole.
I clutched the muddy walls to break my fall.
They crumbled at my weight. Each time I tried
to right myself I slipped and fell again.
Ankle-deep in mud, I screamed for help,
struggling in darkness for what seemed like hours,
screaming as I slipped back down each time.

Finally I lay there panting at the bottom.
It seemed so deep I didn't try again,
and, absolutely sure that I would die there,
I fell asleep, still glad that I'd left home.

And I remember waking up that morning
in a ditch beside a cornfield. I
was hungry, cold. My clothes were caked with mud.
The first thing that I noticed was a crow
perched right above me on the ditch's edge,
blinking and crawing at the murky sky.
I lay there shaking, stupidly afraid

the bird would swoop and blind me with his claws.
Trying to keep still, holding my breath,
I watched him pacing back and forth while slowly
the cool green daylight filtered through the corn.

I finally summoned courage to stand up,
and – just like that – the startled bird flapped off.
At first I was embarrassed. How had I
become so terrified of that small creature?
But then I had to laugh. I realized
how many of the things I feared in life
were likely just as much afraid of me.
I knew I could climb out then, and I did –
digging myself a sort of runway up.
Gasping for breath, I knelt down in the field
between the tall straight rows of sunlit corn
and swore I'd never be afraid again.

They found me the next day and brought me home.
That's when I started getting into trouble.
My teachers always wondered why a kid
as smart as me would lie so shamelessly
or pick a fight for no apparent reason.
She wondered, too, – as if intelligence
was ever any guarantee of goodness.

v.

I used to read at night back in my room.
I liked adventure stories most of all
and books about the War – *To Hell and Back,*
The Death March at Bataan. You know the sort.
There weren't more than a dozen books at home,
mainly the Bible and religious crap,
but back in town there was a library,
and it became the center of my life.

The books I liked the best I used to steal.
I filled my room with them – *Pellucidar,*
The Dunwich Horror, Master of the World,
Robur the Conqueror, Tarzan the Untamed.
I didn't want them read by anyone but me –
not that the folks I knew were in much danger
of opening a book which had no pictures.

The more I read the more I realized
how power was the only thing that mattered.
The weak made up the rules to penalize
the strong, but if the strong were smart enough,
they always found another way to win.

Sometimes when she dozed off, I'd slip outside
and head off through the trees behind the house.
She said these woods had been a pasture once,
but now a second growth of scruffy pine
covered the fields as far as you could see.
I had a special hiding place back there.

Near the foundations of a ruined farmhouse
there was a boarded-up old well. I'd pried
a couple of planks loose covering it.
And, if I came at noon, I could look down
and see the deep black sparkle of the water
framed by the darkness of the earthen walls.
At night it was an emptiness of must
and fading echoes that could swallow up
a falling match before it reached the bottom.
Sometimes I'd stretch along beside it,
reaching down as far as I could manage.

I knew there was a boy who'd fallen there.
His family had boarded up the well
and moved away to let the trees reclaim

the fields they'd spent so many years to clear.
I wondered if they'd ever found the body
or if it floated there beneath the surface,
the features bloated like a sopping sponge,
the skin as black as the surrounding earth.

I didn't mention it to anyone.
This was my place. I didn't want it spoiled.
Most people are too weak to keep a secret,
but I knew knowledge gives a person power.
I came there every evening – or at least
whenever I could sneak away from her.

One night I started whispering down the well.
What was it like, I asked him, to be dead?
What was there left without your family,
your home, your friends, even your name forgotten,
the light shut out, the moist earth pressing round?
Of course he didn't answer me. The dead
never do. Not him. Not even Jesus.
Only a razor's edge of moonlight gleaming,
silent at the bottom of the well.

I realized that if he could return,
if he could rise again through the dark shaft
and stand there in the sun, breathing the air,
what use would all our morals be to him?
Death leaves an emptiness that words can't fill.
No, he would seize whatever things he wanted,
and what would guilt or honesty or love
matter to him now? Coming from the dead,
he would be something more or less than human,
something as cruel and hungry as a wolf.

How was I any different from him?
I came to death each day and sat beside it.

I breathed its musty odor in my lungs.
My only luck was that I was alive.

That was the night that I was born again,
not out of death, but into it – with him,
my poor unwitting Savior in the well.
If I could only become strong enough,
I could do anything. I only had
to throw away the comfortable lies,
the soft morality. The way a snake
sloughs skin when it becomes too small, the way
a wolf cub sheds its milk-teeth for its fangs.

The next day when I saw a neighbor's dog
sniffing around the well, I called him over,
let him nuzzle me, and slit his throat.
I stuffed him full of of rocks and threw him in.
I wanted to be sick, but I stayed strong.
Later I killed a cat and then another dog,
and when I heard two neighbors talk about
keeping their kids and pets inside at night
because a wolf had come down from the hills,
I had to smile. My new life had begun.

I started pulling petty robberies,
spaced months apart at first but then more often.
I never got caught though, except by her.
I'd come home late at night, and there she'd be
staring at me, so pious, old, and ugly –
although she didn't guess the half of it.
And things went on like that until one night
they caught me cold, and I still had the gun.

In prison everyone's a little crazy –
nothing to do and lots of time to do it.
So soon you either fasten on some memory
or lose your mind. Most guys just choose a woman
or a special place, but who knows what it takes
to make one thing stick in your mind for years?
Some people there, who barely talked outside,
would ramble on for hours about Sue
or Laurie Jean, Lynette or dear old Mama.
I knew a fellow who talked all day long
about some Friday night five years before
when he'd gone drinking with his older brothers.
He sat there trying to remember it,
putting each scrap exactly in its place –
the car, the burger joint, the brand of beer.
And when no one would listen any more,
he sat at dinner by himself and drew
street maps of his home town on paper napkins,
carefully marking out the route they traveled.
Madness makes storytellers of us all.

I was no different. Think of it this way:
I lay there in my cell for seven years
and stared up at a window blank with sky,
day after day when nothing came in view.
My cell was littered with unfinished books.
The chaplain always complimented me
for reading, but he didn't understand.
The stories didn't matter any more.
I grew to hate them. Writers lie too much.
They offer an escape which seems so real,
but when you're finished, nothing ever changes.
The things I wanted couldn't come from books.

I used to make up games to pass the time.
My favorite was called Roommates. I'd catch
a horse-fly or a cockroach in a jar –
that would be roommate number one – and then
I'd look behind the toilet for a spider.
I'd drop him in the jar and see what happened.
I liked to watch the roommates get acquainted.
Know what I learned? That spiders always win.

At night I tried to keep myself from screaming.
I'd lie there listening to the toilets flush,
the bedposts scrape the floor, the yard dogs howl,
the guards who shuffled down the corridors,
the fellow in the next cell jerking off.
I had to think of something to keep sane,
and so I thought of her, of everything
she did for me, of everything she said.
I looked into my heart and heard a voice.
It told me what I must have known for years –
that when they let me out, I had to kill her.

VII.

When they escape, most guys head straight for town,
steal anything they can, get drunk, get laid,
and then get caught. They don't know what they want.
I knew exactly why I'd risked my neck.

I made it quite a distance before daybreak,
but, when the light came up, I started shaking.
I'd killed a guard the night before. I'd scaled
a barbwire fence that sliced up both my hands
and slithered through a slime-wet sewage pipe.
But I had planned that part back in my cell.
The thing I hadn't counted on was sunlight –

the sun and open spaces... there were no walls!
I had forgotten what the world was like.

I started crying. Can you picture me
standing there stunned and squinting like a mole
someone had flushed out of the ground to kill?
What a damn fool I was – stumbling at noon
in prison workclothes down an open road.
I tried to hitch a ride, and right away
a lady picked me up. She said I looked
just like her son in Tulsa. She talked a lot.
There's always someone stupider than you.
I ditched the car at nightfall in a field,
and walked the six miles home. I knew the way.

I walked up to the house, then went around.
The front door was for company, not me.
I went up to the kitchen porch and knocked.
I was afraid that she'd look old and sick,
that I would lose my nerve, but then she answered,
looking the same and acting as if she
were not at all surprised to see me there.

She looked the same, and yet I realized
that moment how I had forgotten all
the features of her face. More likely I
had never really noticed them at all –
her freckled skin, the bump along her nose,
the narrow tight-drawn lips which formed a smile
that I had seen before, not just on her.
It was the smile I greeted in the mirror.
I never knew till then where I had learned it.
How strange the people we are closest to
become almost invisible to us
until we leave them. Then, on our return,
we recognize the faces in our dreams.

So now re-entering this world, I felt
how every movement touched some memory
the way a person searching through an attic
will thoughtlessly unsettle years of dust
and send it swirling, splintering the light
into a whirlwind of sun and shadow.

How pointless my revenge seemed standing there.
Nothing I did would bring my childhood back.
I saw her calmly then. And all I saw
was an old woman close enough to death.
I had no right to come and stand in judgment.

VIII.

These thoughts took just a moment, then I heard
"I'll set another place for you at supper."
She had a way about her, see? A way
of putting everyone back in their place,
no matter who they were or what they wanted.
She knew that she had won. And didn't care.

That's when I noticed she had set three places.
Reading the question on my face, she said,
"I have another boy who lives here now."
I told her that I wanted to wash up,
but went instead back to the extra bedroom,
and walked right in.

                    I guess I must have scared him.
He was a scrawny kid with short red hair,
not more than twelve with narrow mousy eyes.
He sat there on the rug, his mouth half-open,
his baseball cards laid out across the floor.

I knew the room. It hadn't changed at all.
The air still stunk from every grudging meal.
The blistered paint, the battered bed and desk
still moaned about the cost of charity.
He crouched there looking at me silently.
Watching him tense, I knew how many times
that angry men had come to him before.
He had the wisdom of the unloved child
who knew he had been damned by being born.

I closed the door behind me. Frantically
he gathered up his cards to stash away.
They must have seemed more precious than his life.
As I came close, I didn't say a word
but took the cash I'd stolen from the guard
and held it out, "Leave me alone with her.
Take this and walk to town." He looked at me.
He knew that money never comes for free
but took it anyway and slipped outside.

I walked back to the kitchen quietly
and saw her busy working at the sink.
She must have heard me come into the room,
but if she did, she wouldn't turn around.
And I came up behind her all at once.
Then it was over — over just like that.

I felt a sudden tremor of delight,
a happiness that went beyond my body
as if the walls around me had collapsed,
and a small dark room where I had been confined
had been amazingly transformed by light.
Radiant and invincible, I knew
I was the source of energy, and all
the jails and sheriffs could not hold me back.
I had been strong enough. And I was free.

But as I stood there gloating, gradually
the darkness and the walls closed in again.
Sensing the power melting from my arms,
I realized the energy I felt
was just adrenaline – the phoney high
that violence unleashes in your blood.
I saw her body lying on the floor
and knew that we would always be together.
All I could do was wait for the police.
I had come home, and there was no escape.

· V ·

Beautiful my desire, and the place of my desire.

—THEODORE ROETHKE

BECOMING A REDWOOD

Stand in a field long enough, and the sounds
start up again. The crickets, the invisible
toad who claims that change is possible,

And all the other life too small to name.
First one, then another, until innumerable
they merge into the single voice of a summer hill.

Yes, it's hard to stand still, hour after hour,
fixed as a fencepost, hearing the steers
snort in the dark pasture, smelling the manure.

And paralyzed by the mystery of how a stone
can bear to be a stone, the pain
the grass endures breaking through the earth's crust.

Unimaginable the redwoods on the far hill,
rooted for centuries, the living wood grown tall
and thickened with a hundred thousand days of light.

The old windmill creaks in perfect time
to the wind shaking the miles of pasture grass,
and the last farmhouse light goes off.

Something moves nearby. Coyotes hunt
these hills and packs of feral dogs.
But standing here at night accepts all that.

You are your own pale shadow in the quarter moon,
moving more slowly than the crippled stars,
part of the moonlight as the moonlight falls,

Part of the grass that answers the wind,
part of the midnight's watchfulness that knows
there is no silence but when danger comes.

MAZE WITHOUT A MINOTAUR

If we could only push these walls
apart, unfold the room the way
a child might take apart a box
and lay it flat upon the floor –
so many corners cleared at last!
Or else could rip away the roof
and stare down at the dirty rooms,
the hallways turning on themselves,
and understand at last their plan –
dark maze without a minotaur,
no monsters but ourselves.
                       Yet who
could bear to see it all? The slow
descending spirals of the dust
against the spotted windowpane,
the sunlight on the yellow lace,
the hoarded wine turned dark and sour,
the photographs, the letters – all
the crowded closets of the heart.

One wants to turn away – and cry
for fire to break out on the stairs
and raze each suffocating room.
But the walls stay, the roof remains
strong and immovable, and we
can only pray that if these rooms
have memories, they are not ours.

Back home again on one of those bright mornings
when the city wakes to find itself reborn.
The smog gone, the thundering storm
blown out to sea, birds
frantic in their joyous cacophony, and the mountains,
so long invisible in haze,
newly risen with the sun.

It is a morning snatched from Paradise,
a vision of the desert brought to flower –
of Eve standing in her nakedness,
immortal Adam drunk with all
the gaudy colors of the world,
and each taste and touch, each
astounding pleasure still waiting to be named.

The city stirs and stretches
like a young man waking after love.
Sunlight stroking the skin and the
promiscuous wind whispering
"Seize the moment. Surrender to the air's
irrefutable embrace. Trust me that today
even seduction leads to love."

Too many voices overhead. Too many scents
commingle in the stark perfume
of green winter freshened by the rain.
This is no morning for decisions.
A day to ditch responsibility, look up
old friends, and dream
of quiet love, impossible resolutions.

ORCHESTRA

Climbing the scales three octaves at a time,
I search for you among the high notes where
the tender flute resides. But where are your
sweet eyelashes? Not there.

Then I descend among the sunlit brasses –
their funnels glistening like fountain tips.
I let them splash me with their streaming gold,
but I can't find your lips.

Then daring ever deeper I explore
the depths the elemental strings command.
Their bows will not create a miracle
without your stroking hand.

The orchestra is still. The score is blank.
Cold as a slide rule the brasses, strings, and flute.
Sonorous lover, when will you return?
The orchestra is mute.

(From the Romanian of Nina Cassian)

SPEAKING OF LOVE

Speaking of love was difficult at first.
We groped for those lost, untarnished words
That parents never traded casually at home,
The radio had not devalued.
How little there seemed left to us.

So, speaking of love, we chose
The harsh and level language of denial
Knowing only what we did not wish to say,
Choosing silence in our terror of a lie.
For surely love existed before words.

But silence can become its own cliché,
And bodies lie as skillfully as words,
So one by one we spoke the easy lines
The other had resisted but desired,
Trusting that love renewed their innocence.

Was it then that words became unstuck?
That star no longer seemed enough for star?
Our borrowed speech demanded love so pure
And so beyond our power that we saw
How words were only forms of our regret.

And so at last we speak again of love,
Now that there is nothing left unsaid,
Surrendering our voices to the past,
Which has betrayed us. Each of us alone,
Obsessed by memory, befriended by desire,

With no words left to summon back our love.

EQUATIONS OF THE LIGHT

Turning the corner, we discovered it
just as the old wrought-iron lamps went on —
a quiet, tree-lined street, only one block long
resting between the noisy avenues.

The streetlamps splashed the shadows of the leaves
across the whitewashed brick, and each tall window
glowing through the ivy-decked facade
promised lives as perfect as the light.

Walking beneath the trees, we counted all
the high black doors of houses bolted shut.
And yet we could have opened any door,
entered any room the evening offered.

Or were we deluded by the strange
equations of the light, the vagrant wind
searching the trees, that we believed this brief
conjunction of our separate lives was real?

It seemed that moment lingered like a ghost,
a flicker in the air, smaller than a moth,
a curl of smoke flaring from a match,
haunting a world it could not touch or hear.

There should have been a greeting or a sign,
the smile of a stranger, something beyond

the soft refusals of the summer air
and children trading secrets on the steps.

Traffic bellowed from the avenue.
Our shadows moved across the street's long wall,
and at the end what else could I have done
but turn the corner back into my life?

Dana Gioia was born in Los Angeles in 1950. He received his B.A. and M.B.A. degrees from Stanford University. He also has an M.A. in Comparative Literature from Harvard University. Mr. Gioia is a business executive in New York and a translator and anthologist of Italian poetry (*Mottetti: Poems of Love* by Eugenio Montale, Graywolf Press.) *The Gods of Winter* is Mr. Gioia's second book of poetry. His first book of poetry, *Daily Horoscope* (Graywolf Press), was published in 1986. He lives with his wife and son in Hastings-on-Hudson, New York.

This book was designed by Tree Swenson.
It is set in Galliard type by Typeworks
and manufactured by Edwards Brothers on acid-free paper.

OTHER POETRY FROM GRAYWOLF

NINA BOGIN / *In the North*

ROSARIO CASTELLANOS / *The Selected Poems of Rosario Castellanos,*
translated by Magda Bogin

JOHN ENGELS / *Cardinals in the Ice Age*

TESS GALLAGHER / *Amplitude: New and Selected Poems*

TESS GALLAGHER / *Under Stars*

CHRISTOPHER GILBERT / *Across the Mutual Landscape*

JACK GILBERT / *Monolithos: Poems, 1962 & 1982*

DANA GIOIA / *Daily Horoscope*

LINDA GREGG / *Too Bright to See*

LINDA GREGG / *The Sacraments of Desire*

RICHARD GROSSMAN / *The Animals*

EMILY HIESTAND / *Green the Witch-Hazel Wood*

VICENTE HUIDOBRO / *Altazor,* translated by Eliot Weinberger

ROBERT JONES / *Wild Onion*

JANE KENYON / *The Boat of Quiet Hours*

JANE KENYON / *Let Evening Come*

VALERIO MAGRELLI / *Nearsights: Selected Poems,*
translated by Anthony Molino

EUGENIO MONTALE / *Mottetti: Poems of Love,*
translated by Dana Gioia

JACK MYERS / *As Long As You're Happy*

A. POULIN, JR. / *Cave Dwellers*

A. POULIN, JR. / *A Momentary Order*

RAINER MARIA RILKE / *The Complete French Poems of Rainer Maria Rilke,*
translated by A. Poulin, Jr.

JEFFREY SKINNER / *A Guide to Forgetting*

WILLIAM STAFFORD / *Smoke's Way*

JAMES WHITE / *The Salt Ecstasies*